THE COLLEGE STUDENT'S COMPANION

BOB ROTH

THE "COLLEGE & CAREER SUCCESS" COACH

authorHOUSE®

AuthorHouse™
1663 Liberty Drive
Bloomington, IN 47403
www.authorhouse.com
Phone: 1-800-839-8640

First published by AuthorHouse 9/9/2011

ISBN: 978-1-4567-9985-4 (sc)
ISBN: 978-1-4670-2520-1 (e)

Library of Congress Control Number: 2011915373

Printed in the United States of America

Any people depicted in stock imagery provided by Thinkstock are models, and such images are being used for illustrative purposes only. Certain stock imagery © Thinkstock.

This book is printed on acid-free paper.

A Special Thank You

*I would like to thank Rosanne Spadaro
for all of her valuable suggestions
and clear thinking as I prepared this book.
Rosanne, thank you for your help.*

Table of Contents

The Job Search Preparation System

Introduction:

Why Does This Book Exist?

THE COLLEGE STUDENT'S COMPANION is the student guidebook that accompanies *The Job Identification Machine*™, a system that colleges use to identify hundreds of employment opportunities for students and alumni.

Parents and students know that concerned colleges offer their students two things:

1. An Excellent Education

    - The Learning Environment

    - The Learning Experience

    - Caring and Enthusiastic Faculty and Staff

2. Exceptional Help In Landing A Good Job

    - A Plan of Action

    - Job Search Preparation

    - Job-Related Work Experience

    - Job Identification

If you attend a college that is using *The Job Identification Machine*™, you are very fortunate. That means that your college is actively responding to the needs and wants of students and parents. It also means that your college recognizes that a good education is greatly diminished when good students graduate without good jobs. Fortunately, your college leaders have decided to embrace a system that will enable students to identify and land more good jobs.

This book exists to help students learn what they should do to:

1. Identify and have access to many more employment opportunities

2. Become better prepared for their senior year job search

The machine works best when all members of the college community come together for one purpose, to identify full-time, part-time and summer employment opportunities for students and recent graduates. It takes a team effort to make this happen. That is why all participants must learn about the role they play in helping to make *The Job Identification Machine*™ successful at your college.

Bob Roth's Job Identification Machine™

Chapter 1

New Student Orientation

ALL NEW STUDENTS, BOTH FRESHMEN and Transfer Students, should attend the New Student Orientation Program. In addition to learning about the College's history, the campus, the activities, the rules and the academic requirements, students will begin to hear about The Job Identification Machine™ and what will be expected of them.

Students are expected to embrace their responsibilities and perform them to the best of their abilities. To satisfy the responsibilities of The Job Identification Machine™ and The Job Search Preparation System, students will be expected to:

- Identify a goal - where they want to be in four years

- Select a major - a major that will support their goal

- Develop a step-by-step plan to accomplish the goal

- Perform activities that lead to the goal - classroom, campus, work, community and leisure

- Participate in training - job identification, job search preparation, networking and interviewing

- Work closely with their personal employment coach

- Prepare for the employment search - classes, research, tools, practice, actions

- Identify and submit full-time, part-time and summer employment opportunities, employment web sites and employment agencies

- Rev up The Job Identification Machine™ - active participation and networking

- Celebrate Job Identification and Job Search milestones and successes

Chapter 2

The Job Identification Machine™ - How It Works

Some colleges believe that student job search training, research and preparation activities along with job identification and the job search process itself are to be left to their students. These colleges try to provide students with a good education, but they believe that their responsibility ends there. Of course, most colleges have a Career Services Department. Unfortunately, that office is frequently understaffed, underfunded and limited in resources. Therefore, the quality of their services can be inadequate and the number of students they serve is likely to be insufficient.

On the other hand, The Job Identification Machine™ is a one-of-a-kind system that brings your entire college community together for the purpose of giving students a substantial employment edge when they graduate. This machine enables your college to:

a. Identify hundreds (perhaps thousands) of employment opportunities for students

b. Address the employment needs of students in nearly every major offered by your college

c. Create a searchable database of full-time, part-time and summer jobs for students

d. Inform, train and prepare students for an effective job search

e. Coach students through their semester-by-semester employment plans of action

f. Offer many students some practical, hands-on experience in their fields of interest

Since most students are not very good at finding and pursuing employment opportunities on their own, colleges that embrace that critical need and actively help their students find good jobs will stand out in a very positive way. The Job Identification Machine™ ensures that students have every advantage in their search for employment opportunities.

This does not mean that some students can sit back while others identify jobs for them. The Job Identification Machine™ requires every student to learn the requirements, obtain the training and then participate and contribute with enthusiasm and determination. Only by doing the research, learning the strategies, obtaining the tools, practicing the methods, doing the hard work and identifying jobs can any student find employment success.

All students are part of the college community and therefore part of the team that will operate the machine. By working together, this team can identify hundreds of full-time, part-time and summer jobs that would never be identified any other way. However, to make the machine work, every student must participate and contribute. No exceptions.

Chapter 3

There Is Much To Do

IF YOU ARE ATTENDING COLLEGE with the intention of graduating with a desirable job, there is much for you to do in the coming years.

Students and parents alike are often surprised by the amount of preparation that is required. Each semester, there are eight or ten important actions that students must successfully complete, if they hope to compete for the best jobs. Yes, I said compete. No employer is going to hand out great jobs to average and below average performers.

The best jobs go to the students who:

- Determine what their target employers want and expect

- Lay out a plan that will lead to the desirable goal

- Work, participate and perform each semester

- Build a list of impressive accomplishments

- Excel at something

- Work on Leadership, Communication and People Skills

- Do the research needed to conduct an effective job search

- Gather and perfect the job search tools they will need

- Build and utilize their networks

- Build relationships for references and recommendations

- Offer a positive attitude to everyone

- Conduct a thorough and comprehensive job search

- Give each interviewer a reason to remember them

This is the short list. Other things will be covered later. And so, it should be obvious that it will take a sustained effort to do everything that is necessary to land a great job. That is why I say, "The senior year job search actually starts in the freshman year."

Every reader should take a few minutes to think about the items on this list. It should be obvious that they require a great deal of research, planning, action and determination. Of course, you have a choice. An exceptional effort will increase the odds for success, while a halfhearted effort will almost surely lead to disappointment. Keep in mind that employers believe that your past performance is the best indicator of future performance. When it is time for you to seek employment, what will your past performance tell employers about you?

Chapter 4

Student Responsibilities

STUDENTS WILL FUEL THE JOB Identification Machine™. Since all students have both a need to find a good job and a personal network that they can tap into, there is an extremely high probability that the contacts in their networks will know of or can find out about employers that will have full-time, part-time or summer employment opportunities for college students. Each student has the responsibility to use his/her personal network to uncover jobs, call employers, gather information about each employment opportunity, fill out a Job Identification Form and submit the completed form to the Database Coordinator.

When large numbers of students accept this challenge, many hundreds of employment opportunities will be made known to the students at your college. That means that many more students will have the opportunity to pursue full-time, part-time and summer jobs both within and outside of their own fields of interest. That is why this is a great opportunity for students to take charge of something that is extremely important and can make a huge difference for themselves and others.

Without broad and enthusiastic participation, students will be left to their own devices and efforts. Unfortunately, low or disinterested participation means that many good students will leave college without a worthwhile job, or in some cases, no job at all. However, it does not have to be that way. That is why you and every other student should jump in with both feet and do your absolute best to identify and submit at least one employment opportunity each semester.

It is important to understand that <u>all participants, contributors and students are trying to identify any and all full-time, part-time and summer employment opportunities in every and any major or field of study</u> that is offered by the college.

Students are not simply looking
for positions that would be of personal interest.

In this way, a wide range of opportunities can be identified by every student. Together, when entered into the database, all students can search for employers that seek candidates in their own field of study or broaden their search to employers with other positions that may be of interest. This method ensures that hundreds, if not thousands, of open positions will be identified for students.

I. College Freshmen

<u>Freshman Orientation</u>: During the new student orientation process, freshmen will be told about the The Job Identification Machine™ requirements and the Job Search Preparation Process.

<u>Training</u>: During the first and second semesters of college, freshmen will receive an overview of the job search process and networking. The need for relevant work experience and building a list of accomplishments will be emphasized.

<u>Network</u>: Students in the Freshman Class will be asked to contact everyone in their networks. They will make a list of everyone they know and will be expected to make <u>at least three phone calls each week</u> to identify full-time, part-time and summer employment opportunities for students. A script will be provided. When a job opening is identified, students will complete a Job Identification Form and submit it to the Database Coordinator.

<u>Web Sites</u>: Additionally, Freshmen will be asked to use the internet to identify web sites that will help students identify employment opportunities. When a good web site is found, students will submit the URL to the Database Coordinator.

<u>Parents</u>: Students will be expected to ask their parents to tap their networks at home, at work and in the community. Parents should be seeking employment opportunities for all students. All parents will receive a Job Identification Form, at least twice a year.

<u>Employers</u>: To help others, every student with a part-time or summer job will be expected to discuss the need for additional employment opportunities with their employers. As a reminder, a Job Identification Form should be given to the employer.

<u>Utilization</u>: Freshmen will have access to the Database for the identification of Part-time and Summer jobs.

<u>Coaching</u>: Freshmen will meet with their Employment Coaches twice a year to review their progress and plan their activities for the coming semester. Students should bring their Telephone Call Logs and copies of the Job Identification Forms that were previously submitted to the Database Coordinator.

<u>Job Identification Day</u>: Each semester, one day will be designated as the Job Identification Day. All students will be expected to make a strong effort to find employment opportunities in their own field of study and submit them to the Database Coordinator.

Note: Some colleges may elect to devote a full week to this effort.

2. Sophomores and Sophomore Transfer Students

<u>Student Orientation</u>: During the new or transfer student orientation process, participants will be told about The Job Identification Machine™ requirements and the Job Search Preparation Process.

<u>Training</u>: During the first semester of the sophomore year, students will receive training in networking, along with a review of the job search process. The need for relevant work experience and building a list of accomplishments will continue to be emphasized.

<u>Alumni</u>: Twice a year, Sophomores will be asked to contact members of the alumni community to identify full-time, part-time and summer employment opportunities (An Alumni list and a script will be provided by the Alumni Association). When a job opening is identified, students

will complete a Job Identification Form and submit it to the Database Coordinator.

Network: Sophomores will be asked to contact everyone in their own networks. They will make a list of everyone they know and will be expected to make at least three phone calls each week. When a job opening is identified, students will complete a Job Identification Form and submit it to the Database Coordinator.

Web Sites: Additionally, Sophomores will be asked to use the internet to identify web sites that will help students identify open positions. When an employment web site is found, they will submit the URL to the Database Coordinator.

Parents: Sophomores will be expected to ask their parents to tap their networks at home, at work and in the community. Parents should be seeking employment opportunities for all students. All parents will receive a Job Identification Form, at least twice a year.

Employers: To help others, every student with a part-time or summer job will be expected to discuss the need for additional employment opportunities with their employers. As a reminder, a Job Identification Form should be given to the employer.

Utilization: Sophomores will have access to the Database of Employment Opportunities for Part-time and Summer jobs.

Coaching: Sophomores will meet with their Employment Coaches twice a year to review their progress during the prior semester and plan their activities for the coming semester. Students should bring their Telephone Call Logs and copies of the Job Identification Forms that were previously submitted to the Database Coordinator.

Job Identification Day: Each semester, one day will be designated as the Job Identification Day. All students will be expected to make a strong effort to find employment opportunities in their own field of study and submit them to the Database Coordinator.

Note: Some colleges may elect to devote a full week to this effort.

3. Juniors and Junior Transfer Students

Student Orientation: During the transfer student orientation process, new participants will be told about the Job Identification requirements and the Job Search Preparation Process.

Training: Juniors will receive training in networking, along with a review of the job search process. The need for relevant work experience and building a list of accomplishments will be emphasized. Sales letters and resumés will be prepared. Practice interviews will be offered.

Field of Interest: Twice a year, Juniors will be asked to contact employers in their major/field of interest. When a job opening is identified, students will complete a Job Identification Form and submit it to the Database Coordinator.

Network: Juniors will be asked to contact everyone in their networks. They will make a list of everyone they know and will be expected to make at least three phone calls each week. When a job opening is identified, students will complete a Job Identification Form and submit it to the Database Coordinator.

Web Sites: Additionally, Juniors will be asked to use the internet to identify web sites that will help students identify open positions. When a good one is found, they will submit the URL to the Database Coordinator.

Parents: Juniors will be expected to ask their parents to tap their networks at home, at work and in the community. Parents should be seeking employment opportunities for all students. All parents will receive a Job Identification Form, at least twice a year.

Employers: To help others, every student with a part-time or summer job will be expected to discuss the need for additional employment opportunities with their employers. As a reminder, a Job Identification Form should be given to the employer.

Utilization: Juniors will have access to the Database of Employment Opportunities for Full-time, Part-time and Summer jobs.

Coaching: Juniors will meet with their Employment Coaches twice a year to review their progress during the prior semester and plan their activities for the coming semester. Students should bring their Telephone Call Logs and copies of the Job Identification Forms that were previously submitted to the Database Coordinator.

<u>Job Identification Day</u>: Each semester, one day will be designated as the Job Identification Day. All students will be expected to make a strong effort to find employment opportunities in their own fields of study and submit them to the Database Coordinator.

Note: Some colleges may elect to devote a full week to this effort.

4. College Seniors

<u>Training</u>: Seniors will receive interviewing practice. Sales letters and resumés will be critiqued and polished.

<u>Field of Interest</u>: Seniors will pursue employers in their own major/ field of interest, as well as employers with open positions that may be of broader interest. When they identify an employment opportunity, they will complete a Job Identification Form and submit it to the Database Coordinator.

Although some students may be tempted to withhold positions that are of interest to them, all positions should be submitted to the Database Coordinator. In that way, every student will have many more opportunities. If the employer thinks that someone is right for the position, they will offer the job to that person.

<u>Network</u>: Seniors will continue to contact everyone in their networks. When a new job opening is identified, students will complete a Job Identification Form and submit it to the Database Coordinator.

<u>Web Sites</u>: Seniors will utilize web sites that will help them identify open positions. When a new web site is found, they will submit the URL to the Database Coordinator, so others can use it too.

<u>Database</u>: Seniors will utilize the college database of employment opportunities and employment web sites to conduct their search for employment.

<u>Parents</u>: Seniors will be expected to ask their parents to tap their personal

networks. All parents will be expected to help identify employment opportunities for their own students as well as other students.

Employers: To help others, every student with a part-time or summer job will be expected to discuss the need for additional employment opportunities with their employers. As a reminder, a Job Identification Form should be given to the employer.

Coaching: Seniors will meet with their Employment Coaches twice a year to review their progress during the prior semester and plan their activities for the coming semester. Students should bring their Telephone Call Logs and copies of the Job Identification Forms that were previously submitted to the Database Coordinator.

Job Identification Day: Each semester, one day will be designated as the Job Identification Day. All students will be expected to make a strong effort to find employment opportunities in their own fields of study and submit them to the Database Coordinator.

Note: Some colleges may elect to devote a full week to this effort.

5. Graduate Students

Employers: Since many Graduate students are already working, they will be asked to give their employers a Job Identification Form each semester and encourage them to hire students from their college. When a new opportunity is identified, a Job Identification Form will be completed and submitted to the Database Coordinator.

Network: All Graduate Students will be expected to help identify full-time, part-time and summer jobs for students. When a new opportunity is identified, a Job Identification Form will be completed and submitted to the Database Coordinator.

Job Identification Day: Each semester, one day will be designated as the Job Identification Day. All students will be expected to make a strong effort to find employment opportunities in their own field of study and submit them to the Database Coordinator.

Note: Some colleges may elect to devote a full week to this effort.

6. Part-Time, Night & Weekend Students

<u>Employers</u>: Since many Part-Time, Night and Weekend students are already working, they will be asked to give their employers a Job Identification Form each semester and encourage them to hire students from their college.

<u>Network</u>: All Part-Time, Night and Weekend Students will be expected to help identify full-time, part-time and summer jobs for students. When a new opportunity is identified, a Job Identification Form will be completed and submitted to the Database Coordinator.

<u>Job Identification Day</u>: Each semester, one day will be designated as the Job Identification Day. All students will be expected to make a strong effort to find employment opportunities in their own fields of study and submit them to the Database Coordinator.

Note: Some colleges may elect to devote a full week to this effort.

Important: Students are at the center of this effort. Therefore, every student will be expected to embrace, contribute to, take advantage of and carry out all tasks associated with The Job Identification Machine™ and Preparation For Their Senior Year Job Search.

Chapter 5

The Job Identification
Machine™ Needs Your Network

To MAXIMIZE THE NUMBER OF employment opportunities that will be identified and made available to the students at your college, The Job Identification Machine™ requires the full and enthusiastic participation of every student.

The task of networking is an action that successful job hunters employ effectively. Every employer fills some positions through referrals from employees and other connections. In fact, many employers have an "Employee Referral Program" in which the referring employee is paid or rewarded for the referral. That is why students who fail to network will miss out on far too many opportunities.

Picture yourself standing in the center of a circle surrounded by all of your friends, relatives and acquaintances, approximately 200 people. Then, picture each of those 200 people at the center of their own circles, surrounded by everyone they know. If you were to contact all 200 of your relatives, friends and acquaintances with a question, you would have access to information and feedback from the more than 40,000 people in their networks. That is the power of networking.

You may think that you don't know 200 people, but most students know many more. You just don't realize it yet. So let's see if we can identify the 200 people you know. Start by listing your relatives, friends and acquaintances. Include everyone in the following groups:

High School - Use your yearbook to list classmates, class officers, club members, team members, teachers, administrators, counselors and service personnel. Also include acquaintances in the classes ahead of you and behind you.

College - Roommates, dorm mates, friends, classmates, class officers, club members, team members, professors, administrators, counselors and service personnel. Also include acquaintances in classes ahead of you and behind you.

Local Community - (At Home and At College) Neighbors, Police, Fire, Ambulance, Bank, Hospital, Religious Institutions, Library, Recreation, Accountant, Barber, Hair Stylist, Car Mechanic, Retailers, Business Professionals, Politicians, Community Leaders, City Employees, Village and Town Employees, etc.

Relatives - Parents, Siblings, Close Relatives, More Distant Relatives

Employers - (Past and Present) Supervisors, co-workers, executives, employees in other departments, suppliers, customers and delivery people.

Associations - Local and National Business, Professional and Community organizations.

Military - Active and Retired Military Personnel, Members of the Military Reserves

Internet Contacts - Students should carefully consider using social networking sites, like Facebook® and business networking sites, like Linkedin®, to identify potential contacts.

After you complete your list, you will find that you know more people than you thought. Record their professions and contact information including names, mailing addresses, phone numbers and e-mail addresses. You will also want to keep notes regarding your relationship and any information gathered or exchanged.

The group that you have just assembled is your network. However, to be effective, your network must be cultivated and nurtured. Most of all, your network must be used and strengthened.

"An effective network is the secret weapon of the best job hunters."

-- Bob Roth

College students who create and effectively tap their networks can unleash a plethora of targeted and useful job hunting information. Whenever you need information and contacts for your job search, you would be wise to tap your network. There will be people in your network who have the information and contacts you need. Be sure to use them.

Your network can only work if you contact the people within it. The key to a working network is mutual respect, concern for others and a genuine interest in helping others. Importantly, you must understand that networks operate in both directions. Your goal is to obtain useful information and contacts, but you must also be willing to help them and share information.

Creating and maintaining a network is very difficult, since a network requires constant attention. That means that you must contact and share information with the people in your network on a regular basis. If you only contact people when you need help, you may turn them off. The best networkers take a genuine interest in others. They contact their network just to keep in touch and to see if there is anything they can do to help. Remember, people who help others will always receive more in return.

Since networking can provide critical information about people, employers and job opportunities, it makes a lot of sense for college students to take advantage of this job hunting technique. It works in even the worst economic times and helps to uncover the positions that never get advertised. That's why I say, "To find a great job, build a great network."

When the networking efforts of individual students are combined, it is possible for the students at your college to identify thousands of full-time, part-time and summer employment opportunities. That is the power of team networking.

Chapter 6

Networking Scripts and Forms

To HELP STUDENTS NETWORK MORE effectively, scripts will be made available by your college. Both paper forms and electronic forms will be available for the following:

- When Calling Friends, Relatives & Acquaintances

- For Students Referred To Another Contact

- When Making Cold Calls To People You Don't Know

- The Job Identification Form

As students become more comfortable with networking, they may modify the questions they ask and tailor them to the person or situation. In addition to the forms listed above, students will also use:

- The Telephone Log Form

The Telephone Log Form is used by students to record the names and contact information of the people they will call. It also has a section to record the results of the call or contact.

Chapter 7

Expectations

All students should understand that finding employment opportunities for themselves and other students is only part of what is expected of them. To conduct a successful job search, students should have:

- An Employment Goal

- A Plan To Achieve The Goal

- A List Of Accomplishments That Will Attract Employers

- Satisfactory Grades

- Training In Job Search Tools and Techniques, Including Networking

- A Superior Resumé and Sales Letter

- A List of Target Employers and Web sites

- A List of Reasons Why They Should Be Hired

- Interview Training

- Enthusiastic References

You and the other students at your college will hear about the things on this list, from the very beginning. You will not only hear about your role in The Job Identification Machine™, but also "how to" accomplish the steps above. Your personal employment coach will frequently review this list with you, discuss your progress and offer feedback.

All students must be clear about what it takes to achieve employment success and what is going to be expected of them.

Chapter 8

Student Research & Submission Requirements

ALL STUDENTS, BUT ESPECIALLY JUNIORS and Seniors, will be expected to do several more things. They will be expected to identify:

- <u>Employers</u> that hire new graduates in their own fields of study

- <u>Employment Web Sites</u> that list jobs that graduates can fill

- <u>Employment Agencies and Search Firms</u> that can help to place recent college graduates

Information about potential employers for every college major should be recorded on a Job Identification Form and submitted to the Database Coordinator.

Additionally, information about employment web sites, employment agencies, along with their areas of specialization, should be recorded on the appropriate form and submitted to the Database Coordinator.

Chapter 9

Job Identification Day

EACH SEMESTER, ONE DAY WILL be designated as "Job Identification Day." It is on that day that students in Groups, Clubs, Organizations, Teams, Majors and Fields will focus their energies on identifying employment opportunities in their own areas of specialization, majors or fields of interest.

To make this day as successful as possible, Professors, Group Leaders, Team Captains, Club Presidents, Advisors, Coaches and Career Services will help students prepare in advance. Before the telephone calls can be made, much networking and research needs to be done. Potential employers will need to be identified, including the names and titles of the people they will contact, their address or location and their phone numbers. That all takes time.

Students are free to search any geographical area, including their home county and state, the county and state in which the college is located or anywhere else potential employers may exist. No restrictions.

To make the process a bit easier for students, the following information, training and items will be provided by the college:

- Information on Employer Research and Information Gathering

- Information about Networking

- Training - Observe or participate in a networking call

- Telephone Call Logs

- Networking Scripts

- Job Identification Forms

Once students have the information and forms and have also assembled a list of potential employers, they can begin to call each contact. As full-time, part-time or summer employment opportunities are identified, a Job Identification Form should be completed and submitted to the Database Coordinator.

Note: Everyone should realize that Job Identification usually requires multiple calls and follow-up with target employers. That is because the person who is being called may not be available when the first or second call is made. That means follow-up and persistence on the part of students, over the course of several days or even weeks, may be necessary. It may also mean that students should talk to others within the organization. Since more than one person will have the employment information they seek, students should be prepared to talk with a variety of people in any organization:

- Department Heads

- Department Supervisors

- Human Resources Personnel

- Employment Interviewers

- Campus Recruiters

- Former Students

- Anyone in the organization who can introduce them to key people

To improve student job identification performance, <u>competition</u> between groups will be encouraged. Recognition and inexpensive rewards may be provided to the groups that have the best performance and greatest success.

Note: At some colleges, Job Identification Day may be extended to a full week.

Chapter 10

Employment Web Site Submissions

To HELP IDENTIFY MORE EMPLOYMENT opportunities, students will be asked to identify and submit employment web site URL's to the Database Coordinator.

Over the course of a few years, a wide variety of employment web sites will be identified. Importantly, those web sites can gradually be classified into groups that best serve each of the subject areas offered by your college.

Additionally, there are web sites that specialize in providing employment opportunities for:

- College Students and Recent Graduates

- Summer Jobs

- Internships

- International Jobs

- Federal Jobs

- Green Jobs

- Healthcare Positions

- Sports

- Entertainment

- Information Technology

- Telecommunications

- Accounting

- Sales and Marketing

- Non-Profit Employers

- Newspaper, Radio & TV Jobs

. . . and others

Students should continually look for and submit web sites that can be added to the college's database of useful employment web sites.

Chapter 11

Employment Agencies and Search Firms

ALL STUDENTS WILL BE ASKED to identify and submit the contact information for Employment Agencies and Search Firms that serve the students who will be graduating from their college.

Like Employment Web Sites, there are Employment Agencies and Search Firms that can help students identify employment opportunities in every field of study. In time, students will be able to search the Database for those agencies and search firms that will enable them to find employment opportunities in their fields.

Students should continually look for and submit Search Firms and Employment Agencies that can be added to the college's Database.

Chapter 12

Your Employment Coach

ALL STUDENTS WILL BE ASSIGNED an "employment coach" to help them plan and accomplish the following:

- Develop a step-by-step plan

- Participate in job-related Clubs and Activities

- Gain some relevant work experience

- Build a list of accomplishments

- Learn a variety of job search tools and techniques

- Identify target employers

- Research target employers to determine exactly what they expect

- See and explore their options

- Overcome the obstacles that are bound to arise

- Get answers to their questions

- Build and utilize a job search network

- Prepare impressive examples and stories

- Develop an exceptional resumé

- Create a personal interview strategy

- Practice for interviews by taking mock interviews

- Build relationships with potential references

- Learn how to differentiate themselves

- Stick with their plan

- Obtain guidance, encouragement and support

Getting prepared to find a good job is hard work. It also takes a great deal of time. That is why students must get started early and follow their personal plans during each semester of college. If students wait too long to begin and have no plan to follow, far too many will be disappointed with their job search results.

Who will serve as your career coaches? Generally, this group will be made up of:

- Career Services personnel

- Professors & Classroom Instructors

- Administrators and Counselors

- Others who volunteer or are selected

Chapter 13

Practical Learning Experiences For Students

The implementation of The Job Identification Machine™ will enable your college to develop a variety of learning opportunities for students.

1 - The Student Learning Coordinator

The Student Learning Coordinator will work closely with all of the Professors in majors that will be supporting The Job Identification Machine™. He/she will coordinate the efforts of Professors and students to help them develop ideas, activities and learning experiences that will help to ensure the success of The Job Identification Machine™. The following majors may be considered:

- Information Technology

- Marketing

- Advertising

- Radio

- TV

- Communications

- Theater

- Music

- Any others that are appropriate . . .

2 - Firsthand Learning Experiences

One important goal is to give students some practical, real life work experience in their fields of interest, as they help The Machine get up and running and then keep it running smoothly.

As Professors develop student assignments, they will consider the following:

a. <u>Marketing Majors</u> - Students can develop and carry out a campus marketing campaign to boost student participation.

b. <u>Advertising Majors</u> - Advertising students can create an exciting advertising campaign for The Student Job Identification Machine™.

c. <u>Information Technology</u> - Information Technology students can be instrumental in creating the database that will list all full-time, part-time and summer employment opportunities. IT students can also help to develop the Job Identification web site to post information, pictures, goals, incentives, performance statistics and exciting news.

d. <u>The Arts</u> - Music, Theater and Arts students can develop some form of entertainment for a Job Identification rally or to celebrate successes and milestones at the end of each semester.

e. <u>Business Majors</u> - Students in this group can administer the budget, gather and analyze the performance statistics and generate ideas to encourage student participation and performance.

f. <u>Journalism</u> - Journalism students and the Campus newspaper can address and write about every aspect of The Job Identification Machine™ and how it will benefit students.

g. <u>Campus Media</u> - Campus Radio and TV stations can run advertisements, interview various participants and discuss the issues that accompany The Job Identification Machine™.

Note: With a little bit of creativity, students in other majors can find ways to use this initiative to gain some experience in their fields of interest.

3 - Other Learning Experiences

Some Professors make it their mission to both develop great students and provide them with occasions to interact with people with contacts in their field of interest.

Wise students who get to know their Professors can learn about:

a. <u>Former Employers and Co-Workers</u> - Many Professors have worked at other places before they came to your college. They may have worked at another college or were employed by a private employer. Therefore, they are likely to still have contacts at those employers. Additionally, most adjunct instructors are currently employed in the outside world. They can serve as great resources for students.

b. <u>Consulting Assignments</u> - How many professors serve as consultants to employers in your area of interest? When professors serve as consultants, they will have contacts that can be useful. Additionally, many professors ask students to help them on consulting projects. Practical experience like that will look good on a resumé.

c. <u>Speaking Engagements</u> - When Professors are called upon to make presentations, they will come in contact with people who can be helpful to students. Many attendees will be from fields that are related to that of the speaker. That means that the speaker will meet people who work for employers in a related field. When students help to set up, attend or participate in these presentations, information and contacts can be obtained.

d. <u>Books and Articles</u> - Many Professors are in the process of writing books and articles on subjects related to their area of expertise. Since they frequently call upon and rely on students to help them with routine tasks, those student helpers will have the opportunity to gain some knowledge and may meet some interesting people.

e. <u>Associations</u> - Professors often belong to a variety of associations in their area of specialization. Interested students may be invited to attend a few of those meetings each year. This can present some great networking opportunities.

f. <u>Research</u> - When professors are active in their fields, they often conduct research and publish papers on their theories and findings. In many cases, they ask students to help them with their research projects. This will give students the opportunity to hear about and meet with other researchers. Firsthand experience, introductions and contacts will all be helpful during their job search.

g. <u>Their Reputation</u> - When students have a class with a Professor who is active in his/her field, their reputation can open doors and lead to contacts and opportunities. By talking with the Professor, discussing their work and looking for ways to help them, students can gradually build a relationship that may be beneficial to everyone.

h. <u>Former Students</u> - Many Professors stay in touch with former students. That is one of the ways they stay up on what is going on in their field. These former students can be very helpful to current students who are looking for employment opportunities.

i. <u>Former College Classmates</u> - Your Professors went to college and graduate school. Many maintain ongoing relationships with their friends from college. Therefore, those old friends may have contacts and information that can be helpful to students who are looking for employment opportunities.

Additionally, Professors can help their students in other ways:

j. <u>Guest Speakers</u> - Motivated Professors invite guest speakers from employers to make presentations in class or in a special venue. This can give students a completely different perspective on their field of interest.

k. <u>Advisory Roles</u> - Involved Professors often serve as advisors for Clubs and activities in their field of interest.

l. <u>Arranging Tours</u> - Professors can introduce students to the workplace environment by arranging for tours of employer facilities.

m. <u>References</u> - Students will benefit when a Professor in their field of interest is willing to provide an enthusiastic reference verbally or in writing.

As students build relationships with Professors, there will be opportunities to discuss all of these possibilities. Do not miss your chance to benefit from those positive relationships. Most will be happy to help you succeed.

Chapter 14

Student Leaders

───────────────────────

STUDENT LEADERS PLAY A CRITICAL role in The Job Identification Machine™. They will be expected to build support, encourage student involvement and create a competitive environment. These student leaders may also help with student training activities, suggest incentives, obtain guest speakers and motivate clubs and organizations to compete.

Chapter 15

Student Employment Progress Evaluation

As you have seen in earlier chapters, there are many things that students should do in order to become totally prepared for their senior year job search. Therefore, your employment coach will meet with you at the beginning of each semester. During the meeting, your coach will discuss your:

1. Job Search Preparation Tasks & Assignments

2. Job Identification Tasks & Assignments

3. Performance During The Prior Semester

During the meeting, your coach will complete and discuss The Student Progress Evaluation Form. In this way, you will see where you stand, so you can stay on top of your employment-related assignments:

1. Identify Employment Opportunities

2. Get Prepared For Your Senior Year Job Search

When students are not prepared to conduct an effective job search and do not know where the jobs are, they stand little chance of finding employment success.

The Job Search
Preparation System

Chapter 16

Job Search Preparation - Your Plan

THERE IS A LOT FOR students to know and do before they can conduct an effective job search. Even with the Job Identification Machine™ available to uncover employment opportunities, a student who is unprepared to give employers what they need and expect will be left out in the cold.

Job search preparation requires a four year plan.

a. Freshmen should:

- Select a career direction as early as possible.

- Conduct Research - What exactly do employers in their field want and expect from candidates?

- Identify influential people who can help them.

- Build credibility with high performing students and influential people.

- Volunteer for something that will help them learn more about or gain experience in their area of interest.

- Get to know Professors, Advisors and Career Services staff.

- Research Campus, Community and Work opportunities.

- Understand themselves and the strengths they bring to the table.

- Pay attention to their attitude and body language. They show others who they are.

- Evaluate their Leadership, Communication and People skills.

- Tend to their grades. Good grades open doors to more employers.

- At the end of the first semester, begin to look for a summer job. They should utilize the Database of Employment Opportunities. Additionally, their personal networks will contain more information and contacts.

- Recognize that the senior year job search actually starts in the freshman year.

- Understand that employers expect a four year effort. Nobody can do everything in the senior year.

b. Sophomores should:

- Select a tentative major, if it has not already been done. As students take their classes and participate in career related activities, they can decide if this is the right direction for them.

- Update and expand their plan of action.

- Begin to create their network. Continue to build relationships with influential people.

- Continue to build credibility with Professors and high performing students.

- Get involved with something in their area of interest.

- Continue to visit and get to know Professors, Advisors and Career Services staff.

- Participate in Campus, Community and Work opportunities. If students do not participate, they will have few accomplishments to present on their resumés.

- Seek part-time and/or summer jobs in their field of interest.

- Understand themselves - What are their interests, strengths and weaknesses?

- Present the Attitude and Body Language that will help them make a good impression.

- Find ways to strengthen their Leadership, Communication and People Skills.

- Identify and research potential employers and job hunting web sites in their field of interest.

- Begin to build a list of accomplishments in their areas of interest and strength. Employers expect to see examples of what students can do.

- Keep their grades up.

c. Juniors should:

- Update and expand their plan of action. Make the goals specific.

- Strive to achieve one or two significant accomplishments that will meet or exceed interviewer/employer expectations. These are the things that will be highlighted on their resumés.

- Continue to build relationships with influential people to expand their networks.

- Do something specific to build credibility with Professors and high performing students. Find ways to help them achieve their own goals.

- Volunteer for something that is important in their area of interest.

- Work closely with their Professors, Advisors and Career Services staff.

- Play a leadership role in at least one Campus, Community or Work opportunity.

- Continue to work at part-time and/or summer jobs in their field of interest.

- Understand themselves - Focus on their strengths and interests.

- Improve their attitude. Present a positive "can do," "let's give it a try" attitude.

- Be certain that their body language and actions match their words.

- Demonstrate their Leadership, Communication and People Skills.

- Identify and research potential employers, alumni and employment web sites in their fields.

- Draft their resumés Emphasize accomplishments in their fields of interest.

- Develop and practice their interviewing skills, keeping the following in mind:

  • What they have accomplished

  • Have examples ready

  • Why employers should hire them

  • Stories about their experiences

  • Questions they will ask

  • What makes them special?

- Meet with Career Services to see if they are allowed to sign up for campus interviews. If yes, get some interviewing experience. Practice telling interesting stories about their experiences or how their accomplishments came about.

- Think about references and recommendations: Identify the most influential and respected people who will speak highly of them. Strengthen these relationships.

- Keep their grades up.

d. Seniors should:

- Finalize and follow their plan of action for year four.

- Keep their grades up.

- Finalize their resumé. Their resumé should emphasize their accomplishments and clearly differentiate them from other candidates.

- Prepare for interviews. Anticipate and practice responses. Develop thoughtful questions.

- Sign up for and participate in campus interviews. Be ready with examples and stories that will impress employers.

- Tap all of their networking sources for useful information, additional contacts and job leads.

- Keep organized and detailed records of their contacts, conversations, promises and due dates.

- Contact every employer in their field, as identified in their earlier research.

- Start utilizing appropriate employment web sites.

- Seek references and recommendations from the most influential people in their networks.

- Conduct a thorough job search campaign. Plan to contact 200+ employers.

Chapter 17

Select Your Career Direction

SOME STUDENTS ENTER COLLEGE WITHOUT a career direction and cannot select a major. However, students often know more than they think. That is because they know what they like and dislike. They can also remember their past successes and failures. Therefore, through the process of elimination, many students can narrow their options down to a manageable few.

Students should first select one or two broad, general areas that align with their strengths and interests:

1. Business - Business Administration, Management, Economics, Marketing, Accounting, Human Resources

2. Computers - Technology, Design, Programming, Gaming, Database, Business & Scientific Applications

3. Engineering - Chemical, Electrical, Mechanical, Civil, Aerospace, Robotics

4. Science - Chemistry, Biology, Physics, Environmental Science

5. Math - Actuarial Science, Statistics, Scientific, Computer & Engineering Applications

6. Humanities - English, Literature, History, Languages

7. The Arts - Art, Music, Dance, Theater, Performance Arts, Film Making

8. Social Science - Sociology, Psychology, Social Services

9. Communications - Broadcasting, Journalism, Writing, Public Relations, Advertising

10. Teaching - K-3, Primary/Elementary, Middle or High School, College, Physical Education, Math, Science, Reading, English, Special Ed, Guidance, School Administration

11. Law - Political Science, Pre-Law

12. Medicine - Pre-Med, Dentistry, Nursing

Once you select an area of interest, do some research. Use your favorite search engine to identify the various jobs that exist in that field. All you have to do is type, "What jobs exist for Communications majors?" or any other major. Some Colleges and Universities already provide information like that on their web sites.

By modifying the original search question in various ways, you will gradually find the jobs that exist for students who graduate with the major you are considering. Knowing what you like and what your strengths are should help you gravitate to a short list of jobs that you can target.

Additionally, it can be helpful to visit your Career Services department to learn about the assessment instruments that they provide in their office. If they do not provide that service to students, they can refer you to someone who can help you.

Some students can begin to understand their operating style by using this simple, self-evaluation tool. For each item below, circle the word(s) that describe you best.

1. Individual or Group activities

2. Indoor or Outdoor activities

3. Fixed Location or Travel

4. Independent or Dependent

5. Leader or Follower

6. Prefer People or Things

7. Quality or Quantity

8. One Right Answer or Many

9. Dictator or Consensus Builder

10. Positive or Negative

11. Exact or Sloppy

12. Does More Than Required or Less

13. Says I'll Do Whatever it Takes or It's Not My Job

14. Accepts Responsibility or Shirks It

15. Helps Others or Watches Them Struggle

16. Angers Easily or Seldom Angry

17. Perseveres or Gives Up Quickly

18. Trustworthy or Not Trustworthy

19. Handles Pressure Well or Does Not Handle Pressure Well

20. Produces A High Volume Of Work or Low Volume

21. Produces High Quality Work or Low Quality

22. Determined To Succeed or Not Very Determined To Succeed

23. Willing To Earn Success or Entitled To Success

24. Giver or Taker

When students understand their own operating styles and select a career direction and field of study that complements their strengths, they can more effectively research the jobs that have requirements of a similar nature.

Keep in mind that nearly every field of study has a business component. Therefore, you may not want to go into Pharmaceutical Research, but might consider becoming an Accountant, Sales Rep, Human Resources Assistant or an Inventory Planner in the Pharmaceutical Industry.

The earlier you select a major and research the jobs in that field, the more time you have to acquire the knowledge, skills, activities, experiences and accomplishments that your target employers will expect employment candidates to have.

Chapter 18

Will Your Performance Impress Employers?

YOU ARE IN COLLEGE TO:

- Gain knowledge

- Gain experience

- Demonstrate your capabilities

If you do not accomplish those three things, employers will have little interest in you. However, you can accomplish these three things by:

- Participating in a variety of on-campus and off-campus activities

- Excelling at something that will impress employers

- Having others say or write good things about you

For most students, there are only five places where they can impress employers.

- The Classroom

- Campus Activities

- The Community

- At Work

- Leisure Activities

You impress employers with your demonstrated knowledge and skill in areas that are important to them:

- Grades

- Communication Skills

- Propensity to Exceed Expectations

- Research

- Thinking Skills

- Recommendations

- Successes

- Accomplishments

- Experiences

- Personal Qualities - Integrity, Honesty, Concern for Others

- Leadership Ability

- Work Ethic

- Problem-Solving Skills

- Ability to Prevent Problems

- Capability to Improve Speed and Save Time

- Knack for Overcoming Obstacles

- Ability to Save the Company Money

- Capacity to Generate Cash Through Sales or Fund Raising

- Creativity

- Technical Skills

- Effort and Determination

- Teamwork

- Relationship Building Skills

- Willingness to Accept Responsibility

- Ability to Get The Job Done

- Skill with Technology

- Positive Impact on People and Projects

- Ability to Make Things Better

- Customer Service

- Reasonable Risk Taking

- Ability to negotiate win-win scenarios

Every student must accept the fact that they will have to compete for interviews and job offers, but not everyone will get the ones they want. Students compete by performing well and demonstrating their competency in the areas that are important to their target employers. We often compete by being or doing:

- More

- Better

- Faster

- Effective

- Different

During the college years, the best students:

- Learn, grow and mature

- Focus on their strengths and interests

- Perform well

- Gain some practical experience

- Accomplish something

- Stand out in a positive way

- Focus on employer needs and expectations

- Get prepared to describe and explain their positive results

- Develop stories and examples that show how and why you achieved results

- Answer questions in a knowledgeable and confident manner

- Ask questions that show their interest in the job, the company and in contributing to the success of the employer

- Know why they should be hired

- Are prepared to address and counter their mistakes and failures

When available, it can also be helpful for students to:

- Provide supporting evidence, documents and articles

- Mention names of people who can verify their performance and results

If you are going to convince an employer to hire you, you will need to:

- Conduct some research to understand the employer's problems or needs

- Show the employer how you can solve their problem or satisfy their need

Chapter 19

Classroom Performance

To HELP ENSURE THAT YOU do your best in class, consider the following;

- Attend every class

- Sit up front

- Keep your cell phone off and out of sight

- Participate by asking questions, answering questions, adding information and by commenting on other statements and questions

- Read every assignment

- Take good notes

- Identify the most important material

- Outline the material you want to remember

- Study from your outline

- Identify the things that you don't understand and get help

- Devote enough time to your studies

- Be prepared for pop quizzes

- Recognize the importance of class presentations. Make them special.

- Do a great job with your research.

- Start and finish papers early. Have a top student review it.

- When appropriate, use demonstrations, slides, handouts, displays and examples

- Associate with the best students

- Volunteer to lead a group project

- Be a great team member

- Show interest in what the Professor is doing on his/her own

- Talk with Professors before and after class

- Volunteer to help with their work, books, papers, consulting assignments

- Think positive differentiation. Find a way to stand out.

What is your learning attitude? If you strive to exceed expectations, your chances for success improve dramatically. However, when you try to avoid the work and fail to put in the time and effort that is needed, you will be certain to fall short.

Chapter 20

Campus Activities

TAKE YOUR PICK. EVERY COLLEGE offers a wide variety of campus activities and organizations in which students can participate. Some activities are just plain fun. Others have the potential for improving student chances of employment success. That is because they offer opportunities for students to learn, grow, experience, practice, experiment, lead and achieve the positive results that employers will want to hear about.

Participating in any campus activity is good. However, playing a leadership role in a job-related activity or organization, and making it more successful, is better. Remember this natural sequence. As you move up this ladder, it is more and more likely that employers will have an interest in you.

- Participate

- Participate in activities related to your field of study

- Participate in job-related activities and organizations

- Accept responsibilities within those activities and organizations

- Lead an activity

- Lead an organization

- Accomplish something important

- Make something better

- Become instrumental in making the activity or organization successful

- Receive recognition for your performance within an activity or organization related to your field of study

Chapter 21

Community Activities

EMPLOYERS VALUE STUDENTS WHO PARTICIPATE in and make positive contributions to the local community. Literally, there are thousands of ways that students and student organizations can make a positive difference in their community. Students can help with or lead any of these community activities and more:

- Cleanup Activities

- Community Gardens

- Teaching

- Tutoring

- Mentoring

- Coaching

- Day Care

- Talent Development

- Fund Raising

- Entertainment

- Athletic Activities

- Senior Citizen Activities

- Music and Dance

- Building Repairs

- Art Shows

- Concerts

Like campus activities, there is a progressive hierarchy of contributions that students can make. The higher the level of responsibility that students take on (participate, organize or lead) and the more success they have, the greater interest employers will have.

Chapter 22

Work Activities

WHILE IN COLLEGE, MANY STUDENTS need to work in part-time or summer jobs to help pay for college. Other students work because they know that work is an opportunity for them to demonstrate their capabilities.

All students should remember that employers love students who have been successful in their previous jobs, especially jobs that are closely related to their own field of interest. That is because employers believe that past performance is the best indicator of future performance. Therefore, it is important for students to understand that their on-the-job performance matters greatly and will either help them or hurt them, when they seek future employment.

Part-time and summer jobs provide opportunities for students to:

- Learn new things

- Demonstrate their capabilities

- Obtain training

- Make something better

- Contribute to the success of the organization

- Build relationships

- Network

- Gain experience

- Develop potential references

- Work as a team

- Build a reputation

- Develop new skills

- Lead a project

- Solve problems

- Demonstrate creativity

- Improve their communication skills

- Get some feedback on their performance

During interviews, when students are asked about their accomplishments, successes and positive results, interviewers will expect students to provide responses that address the items on the list above. In most cases, the effort and enthusiasm that students put into their work will be rewarded many times over. Students who fail to understand that a part-time or summer job is much more than a few dollars in their pockets will come up short with most employers.

Chapter 23

Leisure Activities

WISE STUDENTS ALWAYS REMAIN ON the lookout for opportunities that can impress potential employers. That is why students should take a close look at their leisure activities. When students are skilled, creative and talented, those things are often expressed in their hobbies and leisure activities.

In some cases, a student's hobbies and leisure activities will lead to a great job, one that they will love. Talented students should always consider that possibility.

What have you created, designed, built or repaired? Maybe you do one of the following:

- Take Photographs

- Design Jewelry

- Make Beer

- Cook

- Make Dresses

- Create Stuffed Animals

- Sell Antiques

- Fix Cars

- Build Cabinets

- Love Animals

- Teach Dancing

- Repair Computers

- Design Video Games

- Garden

- Bowl

- Collect Old Watches

- Volunteer In The Community   . . . etc.

All of these examples and many more can impress employers in related fields and may lead to an employment opportunity.

Chapter 24

Where Will Your College Major Take You?

BEFORE STUDENTS SETTLE ON A college major, they should ask and answer five questions.

1. Does your college major lead to a job that pays well and has career potential?

2. With the major you have selected, what kind of jobs are you most likely to obtain when you graduate?

3. Which employers offer those jobs?

4. What do those employers want and expect from students interviewing for those jobs?

5. What should you do during the college years to get prepared for those jobs and those interviews?

Most students do not attend college with the goal of graduating with a job that will ensure that they live in poverty. That is why savvy students select a major and an employment direction that will give them a clear target at which to aim.

It does not make sense to wait until the senior year to identify a direction and goal. The best students know that these steps must be completed as early as possible, so they can spend three full years doing the things that their target employers want and expect to see on their resumés.

By effectively using the larger search engines, you can explore the internet to find the answers you need. All it takes is a little time and effort. Do it today. This is not something that can wait.

Chapter 25

Everything Hinges On Preparation

HIDDEN WITHIN EVERYTHING WE DO successfully is the need for preparation. Even the most talented people don't usually "wing it." They understand and appreciate the need for patience, preparation and practice. That is what makes them more successful than most.

Students who choose to ignore this requirement will have sacrificed much more than they understand. They would be wrong if they would believe that success comes easier for others. It doesn't! Successful people are not deceived by such thoughts and value the benefits of clear thinking, preparation and hard work.

With regard to preparation, shortcuts usually lead to shortcomings.

-- Bob Roth

There is no substitute for preparation, only degrees of it. Students are free to decide how much they will prepare. They can choose not to prepare at all, prepare just a little, prepare to the degree that they believe to be just right or they can prepare far more than needed and waste their time. If we assume that "not at all" is at one end of the spectrum and "far more than needed" is at the other end, then "just right" is somewhere in the middle. Unfortunately, "just right" is different for each student and each subject or goal. However, "not at all" is rarely the best option.

Students should prepare for:

- Classroom participation

- Tests, Quizzes and Final Exams

- Presentations

- Papers

- Labs

- Employment Searches

- Interviews

- Careers

Preparation can include:

- Planning

- Reading

- Studying

- Research

- Information Gathering

- Evaluating Options

- Seeking Advice

- Practice

- Anticipating

- Learning

- Doing

- Working

- Leading

- Communication

- Building Relationships

- Accepting Responsibility

- Accomplishments

- Risk Taking

- Successes and Failures

- Positive Results

- Experience

- Participation

- Networking

- Drafting and Revising

- Building Self-Confidence

Preparation for success in life takes a great deal of time and effort. College is an important part of that preparation.

Too many otherwise capable students look for shortcuts, substitutes and alternatives to preparation, because they are unwilling to spend the time and do the hard work that is required. Since some goals require a long-term commitment, this becomes a problem for students who are unwilling to do the prep work. This is especially true when it comes to the senior year job search.

The senior year job search involves many things that require sustained preparation, over a long period of time. Classroom performance, campus activities, work experience and community activities all contribute the the student's list of accomplishments that are described on their resumé and discussed during interviews. Even the research needed to identify potential employers, career web sites, college alumni and employment agencies or to create a network of contacts requires preparation, time and effort.

Anticipation allows students to see the issues before they arrive. That gives someone the opportunity to get ready for the action or event. This preparation helps to ensure survival. When someone is unprepared for what is coming, they are dramatically hurting their performance. They reduce their chances of doing what is necessary to move them toward their goals and leave them better off.

An exceptional challenge is no match for exceptional preparation.

-- Bob Roth

People do not get better at something by avoiding it. They work hard to get better through analysis, study and practice. It is called preparation. That is what the professional athletes do. They practice hard and hone their skills. They know that they will improve their chances of winning, when they prepare to win.

Most students try to do two things while they are in college:

1. Obtain a good education

2. Graduate with a good job

It is no coincidence that both require preparation.

Chapter 26

Seven Reasons
Why College Grads Can't Find A Job

APPROXIMATELY 3.5 MILLION STUDENTS GRADUATE from college each year. However, most people don't realize that more than a million of these students fail to find a good job, a job that pays well and has career potential. In fact, in tough times, the number of unemployed or underemployed college graduates can easily approach two million.

Importantly, there are clear and specific reasons why so many college seniors and recent graduates can't find a good job. Let me share some of them with you:

1. Beliefs and Expectations

Many students expect to receive a job offer, as the result of campus interviews. The truth is that very few students receive job offers from campus interviews. Therefore, if students aren't well prepared to conduct a strong and competitive job search, over a long period of time, they will be disappointed and frustrated.

Some students believe that finding a job will be easy. They think that they will send out ten or twelve resumes, take a couple of interviews and someone will offer them a good job. They are wrong. All students, even the best students, must compete for the good jobs. In tough times, when few jobs exist, the competition will be even greater. That means that even the best students may very well have to send out hundreds of resumés and take numerous interviews before they receive a decent job offer.

Students often believe that they can wait until the second semester of their senior year to start thinking about their job search. Not true. Everything that students do throughout the college years should support their job search goals. When students ignore the requirement for strong, long term preparation, they will lose out to better prepared students.

2. Grades

Employers tend to have performance requirements. If a student's cumulative average meets or exceeds the employer's requirements, the student may or may not be interviewed. However, if students don't meet employer requirements, they will definitely not be interviewed. Furthermore, when there are many candidates, employers will often increase their minimum requirements.

Many employers use a CUM of 3.0 (B Average) as their minimum requirement. Other employers may have even higher requirements. Students with a 2.5 or lower average may find themselves lumped together with others in the lower third of their class. How many employers actively seek graduates from the lower third of the class? Not many, if any at all.

3. Communication Skills

Some students enter college with poor communication skills (reading, writing and speaking) and do little to improve those skills during the college years. The best employers are not interested in students whose poor communication skills (Limited Vocabulary, Incorrect Grammar, Slang, Curses and Childish Language) will harm the company's image or interfere with job performance. Above average communication skills will impress employers. Poor communication skills will turn them off. It is as simple as that.

4. Work Experience

Employers love students who have been successful in the work environment. When students have been successful in a job that is directly related to the employer's field of interest, that is a very important plus. Even work experience in a non-related field can work in the student's favor when they have made significant contributions and have a variety of successes. However, students who have no work experience whatsoever will usually be considered unproven entities. Many employers are not willing to take a chance on a student who has completed college without having been successful in a part-time or summer job.

5. Accomplishments and Results

The best employers put a great deal of stock in the results that students achieve in the classroom, on campus, at work, in the community and within their leisure activities. When those results are strong, positive and can be tied directly to the job for which the student is applying, that is a strong recommendation. However, when students have average results, no results, or results that are completely unrelated to their business environment, employers will find it hard to see a reason to go forward. Stronger candidates will win out.

6. References

When a well known, highly respected, powerful person provides a strong and enthusiastic reference, employers will be impressed. However, the best references will not provide a strong personal endorsement if they do not know the student very well, haven't seen many outstanding results or have had bad experiences with the student. References are not an afterthought, they are a critical part of the job search and must be cultivated and strengthened throughout the college years.

7. Preparation

Preparation for the senior year job search should be a serious, well thought out, four year process, not a casual, last minute activity. Since most students get started too late, they cannot meet employer expectations and requirements. In fact, most students never bother to identify the expectations and requirements of the employers they intend to pursue. When students don't know what employers want and need, they are highly unlikely to satisfy those requirements. That's a big mistake.

Only students who understand what has to be done and diligently perform the preparation steps, as they go through college, will improve their chances for job hunting success. No student can wait until the senior year of college to try to do the things that should have been done in earlier years and expect to receive a great job offer.

The fact remains that employers offer the best jobs to the students who have earned them. Students earn those jobs with a long series of actions, successes and accomplishments in the classroom, on campus, at work, in the community and in leisure activities. They give their target employers exactly what they need and want. To do this, a student's preparation must be well-planned, methodical, comprehensive and based on employer needs and expectations. When students complain that they can't find a job, it's very likely that those students have ignored many of these seven requirements.

Chapter 27

Your Future Is Not A Gift

Some students waste their time and money in college. They fail to take advantage of the opportunity to prepare for a career. These immature and unfocused students prefer to do as little as possible, skip classes, avoid responsibility and look for the shortcuts. They aren't trying to impress anyone and don't care about the future that they are creating for themselves. However, that approach only works if those students won't need to earn a living and are planning to mooch off their Mommy and Daddy for the foreseeable future.

Mature, focused and clear thinking students work hard and try to make the most of their college opportunity. They understand that because nobody owes them anything they will have to earn whatever they get. Students who are concerned about finding a good job after college know that commendable performance during the college years will open the doors to their futures.

To be successful after college, students must earn their way through the college years. This means that they:

- Earn the best grades they are capable of achieving

- Participate in activities and clubs related to their fields of interest

- Find part-time and summer jobs, preferably in their fields of interest

- Build relationships with respected and influential people

- Accumulate several impressive accomplishments

- Demonstrate their leadership skills

- Make something happen

- Impress Professors and Employers

- Excel in something that is important

- Stand out in a positive way

All of these things require forethought, planning, hard work and determination. Employers and others who can make or break your future are interested in your character, your drive and your results. Are you someone who:

- Is going someplace worthwhile?

- Demonstrates integrity?

- Does the best you can do?

- Helps others?

- Makes things better?

- Gets things done?

- Is fair, honest, friendly and likeable ?

- Puts others first and makes them look good?

- Overcomes obstacles?

- Achieves the goal?

> *"The future is not a gift: it is an achievement.*
> *Every generation helps make its own future.*
> *This is the essential challenge of the present."*
>
> -- Robert F. Kennedy

Nobody achieves success, prosperity or victory by waiting for others to do it for them. Ultimately, our own words, actions and accomplishments will determine our futures. To prevent failure, we must put in the time, do the grunt work, get prepared and carry out our plan with all of the energy, know-how and skill we can muster. Whatever our future brings, good or bad, we will have earned it ourselves.

Chapter 28

A Great Network
Is Critical To Employment Success

AT A TYPICAL EMPLOYER, NEARLY 50 percent of their job openings are filled through some form of networking. Those job openings are part of the "hidden" job market, jobs that are never advertised or communicated outside of the company. Students who successfully tap into the hidden job market have effectively eliminated much of the competition. Therefore, if students don't network, they have eliminated approximately 50 percent of their potential employment opportunities.

Importantly for job hunters, the more people who know them, like them and want them to be successful, the easier it will be for students to obtain information about job opportunities.

Your networking skills will either hinder or accelerate your job search.

-- Bob Roth

A Definition: Networking is typically considered to be a meeting or communication where relationships are strengthened and beneficial information is exchanged.

Because they understand the power of networking, savvy students make a special effort to learn about it. There are techniques and approaches that

75

every student should understand and utilize. Here are a few facts about networking:

- The more people we know, the better chance that one of them will have the information we need. Most people know more than 200 people.

- Students should make a special effort to strengthen their relationships with the people in their network who want them to be successful and would be willing to help them.

- There are other, well-connected people who students need in their networks. Students should get to know them better and make them part of their networks.

- It is the person who requests the networking meeting who actually runs that meeting or phone conversation.

- Students will need a script that they can follow, when they meet with or communicate with an important networking contact.

- Students will need a list of questions they can ask and issues they can discuss, in order to obtain the information they will need.

- It makes sense to know exactly what information will help students achieve their goals before they attempt to get in touch with a networking contact.

- When someone asks, "How can I help?" the student should be prepared with a well thought out response.

- When students make the initial contact with someone they hope to network with but they don't know, students need to tell them who they are, how they got their name and why they want to talk with them.

- When students help someone first, it increases the odds that the person will help the student. Students should think about the people they have helped during the past year or so and ask them to help.

- A key to networking success is for students to contact everyone on their list and ask for a meeting. Students should start with the people they know well, then move on to people they know less well.

- To build a networking relationship with someone students don't know well, they must talk with them periodically and get to know them. Students should look for ways to help the contact and let the contact know how they can help.

- Building a network and maintaining it requires hard work and constant attention.

- When someone provides the student with a contact, the student must make that contact and act in a professional manner. That's because the referring person is likely to follow up to see how things went. The feedback he/she receives will affect your relationship and determine if you are offered additional referrals.

- Networking requires good record keeping. Therefore, students must create a reliable system for keeping track of 200 - 300 people in their network, as well as all of the people the student is referred to, perhaps as many as 1,000 people.

Note: Some of the information that follows has been mentioned earlier, however; it is important to include it here.

After they complete the list, students will find that they know more people than first thought. Names, mailing addresses, phone numbers, e-mail addresses and notes about the relationship, their professions and information exchanges should be recorded. The group that has just been assembled is the network. However, to be effective, every network must be cultivated and nurtured. Most of all, it must be used and strengthened.

College students who create and effectively tap their networks can unleash a plethora of targeted and useful job hunting information. Whenever they need information and contacts for the job search, they would be wise to tap their network. There will be people in that network who have the information and contacts that the student needs.

A network can only work if the student contacts the people within it. The key to a working network is mutual respect, concern for others and a genuine interest in helping others. Importantly, students must understand that networks operate in both directions. Not only do they provide the student with information and contacts, the student must be willing to share information and contacts with others within the network.

Creating and maintaining a network is very difficult, since a network requires constant attention. That means that students must contact and share information with the people in the network on a regular basis. If the student only contacts people when they need help, that may turn people off. The best networkers take a genuine interest in others. They contact their network just to keep in touch and to see if there is anything they can do to help. Because they can unleash the power of their network, giving people will always receive more in return.

Your network will carry you to places you could never find on your own.

-- Bob Roth

Since networking can provide critical information about people, employers and job opportunities, it makes a lot of sense for college students to take advantage of this job hunting technique. It works in even the worst economic times and helps to uncover the jobs that never get advertised. That's why I say, "To find a great job, build a great network."

Chapter 29

It's A Sales Letter, Not A Cover Letter

WHEN COLLEGE STUDENTS ARE INSTRUCTED to create a cover letter, they are receiving bad advice. Letters that merely cover or accompany a resumé are nearly worthless. The letter that all students should develop is a sales letter, a letter that will convince an employer that they are something special.

Sales letters present information that is not already covered in the resumé. They clearly demonstrate the student's vocabulary, grammar and writing skills. More importantly, sales letters offer an insight into the student's goals, personality and operating style.

The best employers want to know what makes you special. At the same time, you want to find a way to differentiate yourself from other candidates. Therefore, your sales letter must fulfill both of those important roles. Here are a few ways for you to accomplish both goals:

- Refer to Professors, Supervisors and Community Leaders who speak well of you.

- Mention several interesting facts that you have learned through research and networking.

- Talk about your most impressive campus, work or community contributions.

- Mention something specific that a respected and influential person has said about you.

- Refer to any problems you have solved or prevented.

- Provide examples of your creativity, work ethic or problem-solving skills.

- Indicate your eagerness to make a contribution with this employer.

- Mention a current employee who has said good things about this employer.

- Show that you are familiar with their products, services, goals, finances and challenges.

- Explain why you are qualified for the position that interests you.

- Talk about your job-related campus, work or community experiences.

- Demonstrate your enthusiasm and interest in the company and the job.

Your sales letter must be carefully crafted and revised several times over the course of time. It is always a work in progress. As things change or you receive useful feedback, your sales letter should be reworked, improved and polished.

Talk with six or eight business professionals, community leaders and professors who know you well. Ask them to tell you what impresses them the most about you. Request that they think in terms of your field of interest, your work performance and your most impressive accomplishments. Once you have the complete list, show it to them. See if any other thoughts can be generated. Then, quote the most impressive statements in your sales letter.

As you craft your letter, make certain that it accomplishes several things. Every sales letter must:

- Effectively sell your attributes.

- Be interesting and creative.

- Flow smoothly and have no errors.

- Contain important information that is not presented in your resumé.

- Be written in a way that will motivate the reader to invite you for an interview.

Once you are satisfied with that final version of your letter, give your letter to a number of people with exceptional writing skills. Ask them to provide you with a few words and phrases that will strengthen the message that you are trying to communicate. Then, go back and incorporate some of those words and phrases into your letter. Let it sit for a few days before you look at it again. Then, go ahead and make the final revisions.

Now that you know that a sales letter is necessary to set you apart and give you an edge, never revert back to cover letters. Sales letters tell employers that they have discovered a special candidate, one they are likely to hire.

College students who grasp this letter writing concept and take advantage of it will always come out ahead of those who don't. The most successful candidates understand that they are writing a sales letter, not a cover letter.

Chapter 30

Make Your Resumé Stronger

FAR TOO MANY HIGHLY QUALIFIED college seniors have mediocre or poor resumés. That is because they were never taught how to prepare for and construct an impressive resumé, one that will attract interest from the most highly sought after employers. The key to a great resumé is preparation. So, let's do that here.

Over the course of a week or two, write out the following information:

a. Describe the job that you seek. Prepare a paragraph that includes the type of job that you seek, the expected job duties and possible job titles. If the job you seek is limited to a specific field or industry, state the field or industry.

b. List the most significant accomplishments, successes and results that you achieved in the classroom and in campus, work and community activities. Strive to list at least ten items. Then, gradually identify the items that are the most impressive and those clearly related to the job you seek or your field of interest.

c. List examples of your leadership skills. Have your ever led a group or a team? Have you served in a supervisory capacity? Were you put in charge of a project? Have you given direction to others? Have you served in a teaching capacity? For each example of your leadership skills, describe the positive outcomes that were achieved.

d. List examples of your communication skills. Have you demonstrated exceptional writing, presentation, debating, persuasion, negotiation, questioning or vocabulary skills? When have you been called upon to use these skills? What was accomplished because of your communication skills?

e. List examples of your people skills. Provide examples of accomplishments that resulted because of your ability to attract, interact with and inspire students, employees, supervisors, professors and campus, work and community leaders.

f. How will you differentiate yourself from other qualified candidates? What is it that will make you and your resumé stand out? What is it that you do better than others? Think in terms of more, better, faster, cheaper, higher quality, better service, job-related experience, level of responsibilities held, skills, knowledge, abilities, creativity, references and recommendations, past accomplishments and potential for future success.

g. List your educational information. This includes the name of your college, city and state, your major, year of graduation, overall CUM and GPA in your major.

h. List the courses you have taken that are closely related to your major and field of interest.

i. Provide your employment history. Include the name of each employer, city and state, your job title, dates of employment and a sentence or two that describes your most important duties and responsibilities. Include volunteer work, internships, part-time jobs and summer employment. Note all significant accomplishments.

j. List every activity in which you participated. Include clubs, sports, campus and community activities. Record your titles, responsibilities and accomplishments.

k.   List any honors, awards and forms of recognition. They can be from campus, work or community activities and involvement.

l.   List your computer skills and software used. Make a special note of specialized or job-related software.

m.   List any job-related technology and equipment used.

n.   List your publications, papers presented or assistance provided to a professor who was working on a book or a paper.

o.   List your job-related memberships. Think in terms of clubs, teams and associations.

p.   Did you study in another country? Describe the benefits of this experience. Did you gain a language skill?

q.   What languages can you read, write and speak? How well? Fluent?

r.   List any job-related research projects. Did professors assign projects that gave you some practical experience? Did you assist a professor, supervisor or community leader on a research project? Note any significant benefits.

s.   Go back and make certain that your resumé contains a variety of words that clearly pertain to your specific employment skills, field of interest and career direction. You will need to do that because many employers now electronically scan resumés for key words.

Once you have assembled this summary of your college experiences, you are ready to write an outstanding, two page resumé. Yes, I said a two page resumé. Anyone who tells you to write a one page resumé, when you have this much to say, is sending you down the wrong path. Employers want to learn about your capabilities. Your job is to give them what they want.

The first page of your resumé is the "sales" page. It is comprised of the information that you provided in (a) through (f) above. At the top of page one, provide your name, full address, phone number and e-mail address. Next, state your objective. If you know what you want, state the position title, job duties and field in which you seek employment. Then, on the remainder of page one, list and describe your most impressive accomplishments, experiences, responsibilities and capabilities.

The second page of your resumé is the "information" page. This page is comprised of the information that you assembled in (g) through (r) above. It provides the facts, statistics and details of your entire college learning experience.

These two pages are a concise view of you and your capabilities. However, it is up to you to present this information in the most attractive and impressive way possible. When you are successful in doing that, the most desirable employers will want to learn more about you. That's when you'll be able to tell your friends, "My resumé is better than your resumé."

Chapter 31

The Employment Interview

ALTHOUGH INTERVIEWING SKILLS ARE CRITICAL to employment success, preparation is just as important. When a student is invited for an interview, that is not the time to blow it. They've worked very hard in college, received good grades and conducted their job search for many months. They are so close to a job they can feel it.

Students should be aware of the requirements for interviewing success. To a large degree, they can be summed up in one word, preparation.

The employment interview is a competition
for which college students have four years to prepare.

-- Bob Roth

Interview preparation is what the student does during the first three years of college. Few students will be successful at anything, interviewing included, unless they are willing to do all of the things that are needed to get ready to succeed. All of those things take time, a lot of time. Successful interviewing preparation includes all of the following:

Research

Prior to every interview, students should learn as much as possible about the employer. That includes their products, services, culture, finances, future projections, expectations, locations, executives, interviewers and the department manager(s) in the student's field of interest.

All of that research can be conducted via the internet and through student and parent networking contacts. However, special attention should be paid to uncovering positive information that can be used to the student's advantage during the interview.

Practice

Students must get some interviewing practice, in order to improve their interviewing skills. Since interviews with good employers are hard to come by, this is no time to be unprepared.

It is always best to record the practice interviews. This allows students to view their performance, listen to their words and think about improvements. Since there are so many important aspects involved, it generally takes six or more practice interviews before everything begins to fall into place.

Appearance

The student's clothing, grooming, handshake, eye contact, body language, tattoos, piercings, jewelry, smile and nervousness all have an impact on the interviewer's perception of you. They all contribute to that first impression that every student should try to control. That's because few things are more important than a good first impression.

Communication

The best employers are always on the lookout for people who can read, write, speak, present, question and negotiate better than most. The student's vocabulary, grammar, tone of voice, slang, laugh and body language all contribute to the way the candidate's communication efforts are received by others.

Resumé

A resumé is just a piece of paper, until the student's past performance and accomplishments bring it to life. A powerful and impressive resumé is a necessary tool for every successful job-hunter. Additionally, that resumé must have a clean look, be error-free and spell checked. In many cases, a strong and interesting sales letter will introduce the student to the employer. Both communication pieces must be carefully crafted and should never be taken for granted.

Accomplishments

The student's past accomplishments are at the heart of an interview. Every employer wants to hear about those accomplishments, successes and contributions. Therefore, students should always be ready to discuss their most significant, job-related results.

Success Stories

Interesting success stories are the bait that students can use to attract the attention of the best employers. They describe how the student was able to achieve the impressive results. Not only do employers want to know what was done, they want to know how it was done, the problems encountered and overcome and the effort required to get it done. That's why students must be prepared to describe how they made something better, helped an employer or organization, solved a problem or overcame an obstacle.

Differentiation

When students are able to set themselves apart from the crowd in a positive way, they will stand out. Wise students look for ways to differentiate themselves from other qualified candidates. The best candidates are both impressive and memorable. That combination will work well for anyone seeking a great job.

Questions To Be Answered (See Appendix 2)

Wise students anticipate the questions that may be asked and develop impressive responses. When students identify some of the questions that are likely to be asked, they can practice their responses and make them much stronger. Students who successfully anticipate questions and prepare for them will have the advantage over less prepared students.

Questions To Be Asked (See Appendix 3)

When the interviewer asks, "Do you have any questions?" you must be ready with several questions that demonstrate your interest in the employer and provide you with useful information. Example: What is the best way for me to get off to a good start with this organization? Show the employer that your first priority is to make them more successful.

Parting Remarks

Since one of the interviewing goals is to be impressive and memorable, the student's parting remarks present another opportunity to do just that. The student can leave something behind (a business card or article), ask another impressive question or make a request (perhaps for a tour).

A wise student asks for the interviewer's business card and follows up with a memorable thank you letter. That is a great way to be memorable and differentiate yourself from other interviewees who do not understand the importance of this communication piece.

Students must understand that interviews are a form of competition in which only one person will win. The other candidates go home without a job offer. Students who are unprepared for fierce competition, will quickly lose out to those who are. That is a fact that inexperienced job-hunters must grasp quickly.

Chapter 32

College Students Must Compete For The Best Jobs

IF YOU ARE ATTENDING COLLEGE to make a better future for yourself, there is a question that you must answer. Do you know how to compete for the best jobs? Well, let me give you a better idea of what is needed.

Since recruiters and employers only know what you give them, you must work very hard to give them strong and positive reasons to interview you, refer you on to the next step and eventually hire you. To compete effectively, you can't leave anything to chance.

A Powerful Resumé

Oftentimes, your resumé is the first thing a recruiter sees. It may be read and evaluated to determine if you will even be interviewed. Keep in mind that your resumé is built first with your accomplishments, then with your words. If you haven't been active in academic, campus, community and work activities, you will have few examples of your capabilities and potential. Resumés are less about what you did and more about what you accomplished. Remember too that employers generally believe that your past accomplishments are the best predictors of future performance.

First Impressions

When it comes to your resumé and interview, first impressions count. Since the best employers almost always have large numbers of candidates, they look for reasons to screen people out, not screen them in. Only the final few will be considered.

Let's start with the way you look. You must dress and look as though the job interview is of great importance to you. Be and look professional. If you don't care about the impression you make, you will kill your chances for success. Your clothing, hair, jewelry, shoes, tattoos, piercings, handshake, smile, speech and mannerisms all help to create that first impression. When the first impression is poor, the recruiter will have little reason to keep you in the running.

Well Spoken

What words will come out of your mouth and how will you say them? Recruiters pay close attention to your vocabulary and speaking style. Your words reflect on your education and level of sophistication. When you use slang, mispronounce words or use a style that is too familiar and not businesslike, you will hurt your chances of success.

Significant Accomplishments

Since employers want to know how you can contribute to the success of their organization, they will want to learn about the capabilities that you have already demonstrated. Those capabilities carry more weight when they extend beyond the classroom. Every employer is looking for people who can get things done and have developed communication, leadership and people skills. Anytime you have success in one of these areas, make certain that your positive results are highlighted on your resumé.

Stories and Examples

Your capabilities are more interesting and more powerful when you are able to provide impressive examples. Stories about your accomplishments add realism and excitement. Therefore, wise students spend time thinking about and polishing the stories they will tell, especially the problems they were able to overcome. Employers love students who are willing to fight for success.

Differentiation

Being able to differentiate yourself from other candidates is always important. However, it is especially important when every candidate has the same major, has taken the same courses and has achieved good grades. To give yourself the opportunity to stand out, smart students seek out job-related activities and employment. As students participate in campus, community and work activities, they can gain experience, improve their skills and develop a list of accomplishments and success stories.

Importantly, there is an opportunity to differentiate yourself in everything you do. Think more, better, faster, solve problems, help someone, benefit your employer or a customer, demonstrate creativity or generate revenue, etc.

Be Memorable

If after a day of interviewing the recruiter doesn't remember you, it is unlikely that you will make the list for a second interview. Your resumé and your interview must be impressive and memorable in a positive way. You must leave the interviewer with a reason to remember you.

When the interviewer returns to his/her company office, you should be in the forefront of his/her mind. Use your creativity to find ways to be memorable. Consider these possibilities: 1) Leave them with a vexing question, 2) Ask them to do something for you, 3) Give them something to read or take back with them, or 4) Send them a thank you note. Whatever you do, it should be businesslike, related to your field and memorable. Your accomplishments, if powerful enough, are the best way to accomplish this task.

References and Recommendations

While in college, students should make a special effort to connect with and build relationships with respected and influential people on campus, at work and in the community. Employers expect the best candidates to have previously impressed leaders and professionals in all three areas. Multiple references from a variety of sources are impressive, especially when they provide enthusiastic and specific examples of your accomplishments and capabilities.

All of this is a little like getting your driver's license. You probably thought about driving for a couple of years before you received your learner's permit and eventually your license. You found out what was required. You studied the drivers' manual and perhaps you took a class. You practiced your parking, developed your driving skills and discussed strategies with your parents and friends. When you were ready, you took your written test and then your road test. If you did well enough, you received your license. You did this because driving was important to you.

If it is important to you to land a great job with a respected employer, you should get started early. The success factors described above must be incorporated into each yearly plan of action. You cannot wait until your senior year. Only students who pay close attention to these factors will be able to compete effectively. Even the most academically successful students can greatly increase their employment potential by addressing these key factors.

Are you ready to compete?

Chapter 33

Savvy Graduates Think
Like Their Employers

RECENT COLLEGE GRADS WHO WANT to get off to a good start in their first professional job would do well to think like their employers. Every employer has a variety of needs and wants that employees are expected to fulfill. The best employees recognize those needs and do everything in their power to satisfy them.

> *"If you want to impress your employer,*
> *There are plenty of things you can do.*
> *One way to get some attention*
> *Is to prove they can count on you."*

Employers want employees who . . .

I. Understand The Business

New employees should make a special effort to learn about the products, services, customers and challenges at their new employer. You can't make good decisions and do an effective job, when you know little about the operation. Smart employees study the literature, read the financials and talk with the employees who have the information they need.

2. Achieve Positive Results

When new employees hit the ground running, employers will be impressed. Since you will see things with fresh eyes, you may spot a few areas that can be improved. Speed and quality together are usually well received. When you look for ways to improve productivity, beat deadlines and exceed quality requirements, you impact the numbers and show your employer that you can contribute.

3. Make Sacrifices

Employees who make sacrifices for their employers and their customers are valued. By helping others, putting in overtime in order to meet deadlines and accepting responsibility even though personal sacrifices may be involved, employees demonstrate behaviors that employers value and appreciate. Employees who are unwilling to make some personal sacrifices for their employers often limit their promotional opportunities.

4. Put Customers First

Most employers realize that without customers, there is no business. That's why employees who put customers first and are willing to go the extra mile for a customer are valuable assets. On the other hand, employees who provide poor service, offend customers or harm the company's reputation will be quickly eliminated.

5. Solve Problems

Employers always appreciate employees who solve problems. The willingness to tackle problems along with the ability to gather the information and resources needed to come up with an acceptable solution is a skill that not everyone has. People who accept assignments that are too complex and end up failing will adversely affect the organization. Wise employees know when to ask for help.

6. Treat Others With Respect

The best employees work well with others because they treat everyone with respect and appreciate their unique contributions. Since teamwork is critical to organizational success, team players are needed by every organization. They encourage others, support them and help them succeed. Employees who do not receive the respect they deserve will almost always underperform.

7. Act In The Best Interests Of The Employer

The best employees always act in a way that will help their employers succeed. They work hard to ensure that their employers accomplish the most critical goals. When choices are required, loyal employees anticipate the consequences and always act in the best interests of their employers. Employees who always put themselves first will limit their potential.

8. Accept And Adjust To Changes

You will face hundreds of changes during your career. With change comes choice. You can quickly adapt, complain and slowly adapt or fight the change and never adapt. Generally, those employees who accept the change, adapt quickly and move on will find greater success. Employees who can't or won't adapt become part of the problem.

9. Present A Positive Attitude

The attitude you choose to present to others will either help you achieve your goals, hamper the achievement of your goals or prevent you from achieving your goals. The most appreciated employees choose to present a positive,"can do", "let's give it a try" attitude.

10. Demonstrate Leadership Skills

Leaders move things forward and achieve results. Every employer loves them because they are able to mobilize and motivate others to perform at a higher level. They bring people together to achieve the goals that require teamwork, inspiration and exceptional performance.

Understand The Bottom Line

Everything has a bottom line. Whether they are concerned about financials, productivity, quality, service or results, employers must be bottom line oriented, if they are going to survive. Employees who understand and aggressively pursue bottom-line results are highly valued. Only employers with great profit margins can offer great salaries and great benefits. Therefore, employees who merely show up to collect a paycheck add little value and have little value in the competitive world.

There is a lesson here. College graduates who intend to find success in the competitive world should understand and achieve the needs and wants of their employers. Exceptional employees exceed requirements, satisfy important customers, achieve outstanding results and solve or prevent the problems that hamper company success.

Many college graduates will find it easier to achieve success when they decide to think like their employers and endeavor to make them stronger. Importantly, once students are employed, college grades no longer count. Grades don't help anyone serve an angry and desperate customer or beat a critical financial deadline. Former "C" students will regularly compete with former "A" students and only their current performance and results will matter.

Appendix I

The College Student's Self-Evaluation Tool

IF YOUR MOST IMPORTANT GOAL in college is to graduate with a good job, you may be looking for a quick and simple way to assess your chances. Here is a tool that can help you evaluate your performance and progress in ten important areas.

Rating Scale - For each item, circle the number that best represents your current status. Superior = 5, Above Average = 4, Average = 3, Below Average = 2, Poor = 1

1. **Grades** - Many employers use grades as their initial screening factor. If your grades meet or exceed their requirements, you may be interviewed. However, if your grades fall below their requirements, they will not interview you. Rate your grades. 5 4 3 2 1

2. **Campus Activities** - Employers generally prefer well-rounded students. They look for students who have been successful in a variety of activities. Have you been able to stand out in a positive way? Rate your overall performance and success in the campus activities you have chosen. 5 4 3 2 1

3. **Part-Time Work** - Your work experience has a high value in the eyes of employers. If you have been successful in a summer

job, co-op assignment, internship or part-time job, especially one in your field of interest, employers will take notice. Rate your work performance and experience. 5 4 3 2 1

4. **Community Activities** - Employers often notice students who have made a difference in the local community. Have you given talks, raised funds, taught students, supervised others or in some way made a contribution in the local community? Since community involvement is another way for students to demonstrate their capabilities, rate your performance in this area. 5 4 3 2 1

5. **Leisure Activities** - When your leisure activities contain performance elements that are important to employers, you should include them on your resumé. Have you started your own business, won awards, been written up in the newspaper, served as a leader or had other impressive experiences? Rate your performance here. 5 4 3 2 1

6. **Accomplishments** - Most of all, employers want to learn about your accomplishments. That's because employers hire results oriented, highly effective, hard working people who have already proven that they can get important things done. Rate your accomplishments. 5 4 3 2 1

7. **Leadership** - Employers love students with leadership skills. Have you taken on any responsibilities that enabled you to lead others and demonstrate your leadership abilities, in order to accomplish a worthwhile goal? You can't become a good leader without leading. Rate your leadership skills. 5 4 3 2 1

8. **Communication Skills** - The most effective students and employees have strong communication skills (Reading, Writing, Speaking, Presenting, Spelling, Punctuation and Grammar). That is why the best employers look for examples of your communication skills. Rate your communication skills. 5 4 3 2 1

9. **Job Hunting Preparation** - Effective job-hunters understand that preparation is a critical key to their success. Because preparation involves so much work and so many activities, they

lay out a step-by-step job hunting plan that will take them from the freshman year right up through their senior year of college. Rate your job hunting preparation. 5 4 3 2 1

10. **References** - Enthusiastic, well-known and influential references can seal the deal for you. That's why savvy students start to think about their references long before they are needed. It takes time to cultivate the respect and confidence of the people you will ask to serve as references. Rate your success in cultivating your references. 5 4 3 2 1

Bottom Line - Good jobs are not won in job interviews. They are won long before that. Good jobs go to the students who recognize the needs and expectations of employers early in their college experience, and work hard to improve their knowledge, skills and experience in the areas that will impress their target employers. Students will not receive job offers if they do not give employers what they need, want and expect.

As a concerned student, you can review your numbers in each area and decide on a course of action for the coming semester. If you start now and work diligently going forward, you can improve your chances for job hunting success.

Your Total Score _____

10 - 20 points - You must get serious about these factors. Start now!

21 - 30 points - Much work needs to be done. Get going.

31 - 40 points - Make adjustments to improve in key areas.

41 - 50 points - Excellent job. Keep it up.

Appendix 2

Interview Questions
You Should Be Prepared To Answer

1. What was the single most important idea you contributed to your last job?

2. What have you done in the last year or so to make yourself a better employee?

3. What will your last employer tell us about you?

4. What job-related strengths would you bring to this position?

5. What were some of the suggestions you made for doing things better and faster?

6. Give me some examples of the kinds of decisions you were allowed to make in your last job.

7. What have you recently done to help your employer be more successful?

8. If you see that another employee is having a problem, what is your normal reaction?

9. What are some of the things you have been criticized for in the past?

10. In order to get your first promotion, what approach will you use? Explain.

11. How well qualified are you for this position? Why?

12. How are you different than most other students who will apply for this job?

13. Describe a job-related problem you have recently solved.

14. Give me an example of your creativity.

15. Give me an example of something you were able to make work better.

16. Have you ever been recognized for being good at something?

17. Do you have a "can do", "let's give it a try" attitude? Give me an example.

18. Tell me about a time that you had to overcome an obstacle to get something done.

19. Tell me about your reputation at school, at work and in the community.

20. How do your reading, writing, speaking and presentation skills compare to others?

21. Tell me about a time when you were the leader of a group and accomplished something important.

Appendix 3

Questions You May Want To Ask

ALWAYS SHOW INTEREST AND ENTHUSIASM by asking questions, as you go along. Early in the interview you may want to ask, **"What are some of the most important factors that will determine if a person will be successful in this company?"** The answer you receive may help you to respond to upcoming questions from the interviewer. Other questions include:

1. What would you like me to accomplish in the first year?

2. How do you reward exceptional performance?

3. What career opportunities exist for someone who produces consistently superior results?

4. Why is this job open? (If the former incumbent was promoted, suggest a meeting.)

5. What learning opportunities exist in this job?

6. What "internal customers" does this job serve? When can I meet with them to discuss their needs?

7. In this job, what is the most important change I could make?

8. What will it take to impress my supervisor?

9. Would it be possible to talk with a highly successful recruit from last year?

10. What are the most important duties or requirements for this job?

11. What is it that makes someone successful in this job?

12. What excites you about working here?

13. How can I get off to a good start with my supervisor?

14. What typical mistakes do first year employees often make?

15. What is the primary culture of this company/department?

16. I read that you are experiencing a problem with xyz, would I be able to work on that project?

17. What challenges can I expect to encounter in this position?

18. As a new employee, I know that I will have a lot to learn. Is there some material that I can read to get an early start?

Because you must convince the interviewer that you "can" and "will" benefit the employer, the questions you ask are just as important as the questions you answer. Never ask questions that only benefit you.

About Bob Roth

BOB ROTH, A FORMER CAMPUS recruiter, is known as The "College & Career Success" Coach. While working for several large international corporations, he recruited Technical and Non-Technical students from a wide array of well-known Colleges and Universities throughout the East and Northeast.

Bob Roth's Job Identification Machine™ - Bob has created a system that colleges use to identify hundreds (perhaps thousands) of full-time, part-time and summer employment opportunities for students. The system also ensures that students at participating colleges are fully prepared to conduct a comprehensive and effective senior year job search. *The College Student's Companion* is the book that students use to learn about their duties and responsibilities with regard to his system.

Books - Bob is the author of four books:

> *The College Student's Companion* (to The Job Identification Machine*™*)

> *College Success: Advice For Parents Of High School And College Students*

> *The College Student's Guide To Landing A Great Job*

> *The 4 Realities Of Success During and After College*

Articles - Bob currently writes articles for more than 225 College Career Services Offices, Campus Newspapers, Parent Associations and Employment Web Sites. To date, more than 90 articles have been published.

Blog - His blog at http://collegesuccess.blog.com addresses the concerns of college students and recent graduates who intend to land a great job.

Web Site - Bob provides information and services to students and colleges. To learn more visit: www.The4Realities.com.

Contact -   Bob Roth
              The "College & Career Success" Coach
              The4Realities@aol.com

www.ingramcontent.com/pod-product-compliance
Lightning Source LLC
Chambersburg PA
CBHW021544290526
45785CB00004BA/1505